EYEWITNESS TO HISTORY

MAJOR CULTURAL MOVEMENTS

Inside the

CIVIL RIGHTS MOVEMENT

WITHDRAWN

WE MARCH FOR INTEGRATED SCHOOLS NOW!

WE DEMAND DECENT HOUSING NOW!

WE DEMAND AN END POLICE BRUTALITY NOW!

JUSTICE

 Gareth Stevens
PUBLISHING

By Kristen Rajczak Nelson

Please visit our website, www.garethstevens.com. For a free color catalog of all our high-quality books, call toll free 1-800-542-2595 or fax 1-877-542-2596.

Library of Congress Cataloging-in-Publication Data

Names: Rajczak Nelson, Kristen, author.
Title: Inside the civil rights movement / Kristen Rajczak Nelson.
Description: New York : Gareth Stevens Publishing, [2018] | Series:
  Eyewitness to history: major cultural movements | Includes index.
Identifiers: LCCN 2017016492| ISBN 9781538211533 (pbk. book) | ISBN
  9781538211540 (6 pack) | ISBN 9781538211557 (library bound book)
Subjects: LCSH: African Americans–Civil rights–History–20th
  century–Juvenile literature. | Civil rights movements–United
  States–History–20th century–Juvenile literature. | United States–Race
  relations–Juvenile literature.
Classification: LCC E185.61 .R2355 2018 | DDC 323.1196/0730904–dc23
LC record available at https://lccn.loc.gov/2017016492

First Edition

Published in 2018 by
Gareth Stevens Publishing
111 East 14th Street, Suite 349
New York, NY 10003

Designer: Katelyn E. Reynolds
Editor: Therese Shea

Photo credits: Cover, p. 1 (person) Declan Haun/Chicago History Museum/Getty Images; cover, p. 1 (background image) Warren K Leffler/Underwood Archives/Getty Images; cover, p. 1 (logo quill icon) Seamartini Graphics Media/Shutterstock.com; cover, p. 1 (logo stamp) YasnaTen/Shutterstock.com; cover, p. 1 (color grunge frame) DmitryPrudnichenko/Shutterstock.com; cover, pp. 1–32 (paper background) Nella/Shutterstock.com; cover, pp. 1–32 (decorative elements) Ozerina Anna/Shutterstock.com; pp. 1–32 (wood texture) Reinhold Leitner/Shutterstock.com; pp. 1–32 (open book background) Elena Schweitzer/Shutterstock.com; pp. 1–32 (bookmark) Robert Adrian Hillman/Shutterstock.com; p. 4 courtesy of the Library of Congress; p. 5 New York Times Co./Getty Images; p. 7 Carllwasaki/The LIFE Picture Collection/Getty Images; p. 8 USIA/National Archives and Records Administration Records of the U.S. Information Agency Record Group 306; p. 9 (both) Don Cravens/The LIFE Images Collection/Getty Images; p. 11 Paul Schutzer/The LIFE Premium Collection/Getty Images; pp. 13, 25 Bettmann/Getty Images; p. 15 courtesy of the National Park Service; p. 17 Charles Shaw/Getty Images; p. 19 Universal History Archive/Getty Images; p. 21 Washington Bureau/Getty Images; p. 23 (top) Marvin Lichtner/The LIFE Images Collection/Getty Images; p. 23 (bottom) Keystone/Getty Images; p. 27 Jacques M. Chenet/CORBIS/Corbis via Getty Images; p. 28 Official White House Photo by Pete Souza.

Printed in the United States of America

CPSIA compliance information: Batch #CW18GS: For further information contact Gareth Stevens, New York, New York at 1-800-542-2595.

CONTENTS

Words in the glossary appear in bold type the first time they are used in the text.

THE START
of a Movement

Civil rights **activist** James Farmer, who worked alongside Martin Luther King Jr., stated: *"Racism was the belief that race has something to do with intelligence, character, and morality. Racism was a concept that some races are inferior and others are superior. That's a lie."*

James Farmer

Since the first black slaves were brought to the American colonies in the 1600s, there's been a division between races in the United States. Even after the Thirteenth Amendment outlawed slavery in 1865, **discrimination** continued nationwide. This was especially apparent in the South. By the 1950s, many were fed up with laws separating white and black children in schools, supporting whites-only businesses, and keeping black Americans from voting. They began to organize and speak out, beginning the civil rights movement.

Signs throughout the South stated what seats, doors, and even drinking fountains "colored" people could use. Jim Crow laws made discrimination like this legal.

Laws **segregating** white and black Americans in the South came to be called Jim Crow laws. The first Jim Crow laws were passed in the late 1870s after Reconstruction, the time following the Civil War when the South was brought back into the Union and rebuilt. These laws kept parks, schools, libraries, bathrooms, train cars, and many other places segregated for more than 75 years. During the civil rights movement, however, the legality of these regulations was finally challenged.

MORE TO KNOW

The Fourteenth Amendment (1868) gave African Americans citizenship and equal rights. The Fifteenth Amendment (1870) stated the right to vote couldn't be denied based on race or color. However, the southern states established Jim Crow laws to discriminate despite these amendments.

STRIKING DOWN
"Separate but Equal"

During the early 1950s, the National Association for the Advancement of Colored People (NAACP) was working to end school segregation. The group wanted to challenge a Supreme Court ruling from 1896 that allowed segregation in schools. The decision in the case *Plessy v. Ferguson* stated "separate but equal" schools were acceptable. The NAACP and their chief lawyer, Thurgood Marshall, disagreed; segregation in schools **violated** black students' rights.

Through their efforts, the court case, *Brown v. Board of Education of Topeka*, finally reached the Supreme Court. In May 1954, the court ruled that separate schools were "**inherently** unequal." It was a big win, but Marshall knew the fight wasn't over. *"I'm going back to work,"* his wife recalled him saying after the case. *"Our work has just begun."*

These are the students and parents whom the NAACP represented in the *Brown v. Board of Education* lawsuit challenging school segregation.

THE MOVEMENT
Gains Momentum

Rosa Parks

In 1955, the arrest of Rosa Parks in Montgomery, Alabama, stirred outrage among African Americans. Parks was arrested because of her refusal to give up her seat to a white man on a bus. She later said of her decision to stay seated: *"People always say that I didn't give up my seat because I was tired, but that isn't true. I was not tired physically, or no more tired than I usually was at the end of a working day . . . No, the only tired I was, was tired of giving in."*

Following Parks's arrest, blacks in Montgomery **boycotted** the city's buses. The boycott lasted more than a year. It ended when the US Supreme Court ordered that the bus system be desegregated.

MORE TO KNOW

Dr. Martin Luther King Jr. first became known as a leader of the civil rights movement during the Montgomery Bus Boycott.

Instead of taking the bus, black citizens of Montgomery drove in cars together or walked to work, stores, and schools. The city took notice because 75 percent of all bus riders were black.

Rosa Parks joined the NAACP in 1943 and was the secretary of the Montgomery chapter of the NAACP at the time of her arrest. For months before her arrest, the NAACP was looking for someone to be brave enough to challenge bus segregation. It's likely that Parks would have known this, but she wrote in her autobiography that her refusal to stand wasn't planned. She hadn't even sat in a whites-only section.

In the 1960s, there were bigger, more organized forms of protest. A group supporting civil rights for African Americans called the Congress of Racial Equality (CORE) led black and white civil rights activists on bus rides in 1961 to challenge segregated busing in the South. Called the Freedom Rides, they began in Washington, DC, and often ended with riders being arrested or worse. One bus was bombed as it crossed from Georgia into Alabama. A few days later, a second bus made it to Birmingham, Alabama, but many of those Freedom Riders were beaten by an angry mob.

The Freedom Rides encouraged many people to protest transportation segregation, leading James Farmer to call them *"no doubt the most dramatic and most successful action of the civil rights movement."*

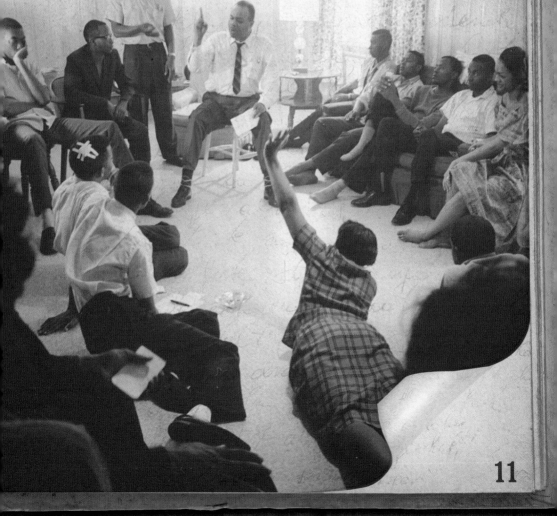

MORE TO KNOW

In 1957, Dr. Martin Luther King Jr. and other activists formed the Southern Christian Leadership Conference (SCLC), an organization dedicated to supporting civil rights protesters and local movements.

A group of Freedom Riders and their supporters were trapped inside a church in Montgomery, Alabama, by a mob. Federal troops had to be sent in to protect them.

THE VOICE
of the Movement

In the spring of 1963, civil rights activists focused their efforts on one of the most segregated cities in the country: Birmingham, Alabama. They organized sit-ins, marches, and other nonviolent protests as acts of "civil disobedience." These were common methods of challenging segregation among civil rights activists in the early 1960s. No civil rights leader was more in favor of peaceful protest than Dr. Martin Luther King Jr.

In April 1963, King was jailed for leading a march after the Alabama state court ruled against protests. He wrote about civil disobedience in his famous "Letter from Birmingham City Jail." King wrote, *"The way of nonviolence became an integral*

CIVIL DISOBEDIENCE AND GANDHI

Civil disobedience is the refusal to follow certain laws as a form of peaceful protest. Mohandas Gandhi used civil disobedience to oppose British rule in India until he was killed in 1948. Gandhi inspired King's belief in nonviolent protest. *"I had come to see early that the Christian doctrine of love operating through the Gandhian method of nonviolence was one of the most potent weapons available to the Negro in his struggle for freedom,"* King said.

part of our struggle. If this philosophy had not emerged, by now many streets of the South would, I am convinced, be flowing with blood."

MORE TO KNOW

Time magazine named King the "Man of the Year" in 1963 and commented about his letter from jail: *"It may yet live as a classic expression of the Negro revolution of 1963."*

This photograph was taken when King (center) and civil rights activist Ralph Abernathy (left) were released from the Birmingham jail.

COULDN'T
Be Ignored

KENNEDY ASKS FOR LAWS

The Birmingham Campaign, as well as the many other protests happening around the United States, convinced President Kennedy to propose new civil rights laws. *"In too many parts of the country, wrongs are inflicted [imposed] on Negro citizens and there are no remedies at law,"* Kennedy said in a speech in June 1963. *"Unless Congress acts, their only remedy is [to protest in] the street."*

Despite civil rights activists' nonviolent protests in Birmingham, their efforts were often met with violence. The police even used fire hoses, clubs, and dogs on protesters. When people across the nation saw press coverage of the events, they were outraged. Important officials took notice, including those in government such as President John F. Kennedy. Kennedy spoke out about what he'd seen: *"The events in Birmingham . . . have so increased the cries for equality that no city or state or legislative body can prudently [wisely] choose to ignore them."*

In May 1963, Birmingham's government officials finally agreed to take down "white only" and "black only" signs, help African Americans find jobs, and release protesters who had been arrested.

14

John F. Kennedy was assassinated before he could see the new civil rights laws come to be.

MORE TO KNOW

Birmingham's desegregation made some who opposed it turn to violence. The Sixteenth Street Baptist Church was bombed not long after the desegregation agreement was made. Four young girls were killed.

THE MARCH
on Washington

On August 28, 1963, more than 200,000 people headed to Washington, DC, for the biggest demonstration of the civil rights movement yet: the March on Washington for Jobs and Freedom.

John Lewis, age 23, was the youngest speaker of that day, but his words had great effect: *"To those who have said, 'Be patient and wait,' we have long said that we cannot be patient. We do not want our freedom gradually, but we want to be free now! . . . I appeal to all of you to get into this great revolution that is sweeping this nation. Get in and stay in the streets of every city, every village and hamlet of this nation until true freedom comes, until the revolution of 1776 is complete."*

MORE TO KNOW

King gave the most famous speech of the day at the March on Washington. He said: *"I have a dream that my four little children will one day live in a nation where they will not be judged by the color of their skin but by the content of their character."*

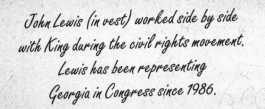

John Lewis (in vest) worked side by side with King during the civil rights movement. Lewis has been representing Georgia in Congress since 1986.

THE CIVIL RIGHTS ACT OF 1964

President Lyndon Johnson, who replaced Kennedy after he was assassinated, signed the Civil Rights Act into law on July 2, 1964. The law barred segregation in businesses and public places such as libraries, public schools, and swimming pools. The act also said it was illegal for employers to discriminate against anyone based on "race, color, religion, sex, or national origin" when hiring. With this statement, the act protected women and people of many races, religions, and nationalities, too.

ENSURING
the Right to Vote

BLOODY SUNDAY

March 7, 1965, is called Bloody Sunday because of the terrible attack on marchers. As they crossed the bridge out of Selma, a wall of troopers waited for them. Alabama governor George Wallace had instructed the troopers to *"use whatever measures are necessary to prevent a march."* When the marchers wouldn't turn back, the troopers used tear gas, beat them, and even chased those who tried to run away.

In January 1965, civil rights groups began efforts to register more black voters in Selma, Alabama. The police brutality in Selma was well known, so it was understood the police might respond with force. By February, violence toward civil rights activists had begun.

A 5-day voting rights march from Selma to Montgomery was planned for March 7. As marchers tried to leave Selma, state troopers and local law enforcement attacked them. The marchers wanted to try again a few days later, but the march was delayed until March 21. When they finally made it to Montgomery, King said: *"The Civil Rights Act of 1964 gave Negroes some part of their rightful dignity, but without the vote it was dignity without strength."*

Civil rights activists were even more determined to march after the death of Jimmie Lee Jackson, a 26-year-old black man who was shot trying to protect his mother from a police officer.

Even though the Fifteenth Amendment gave African Americans the right to vote, many places made it almost impossible for them to register to vote or reach the polls. The march from Selma to Montgomery showed that black Americans wouldn't back down in their fight to vote.

Bloody Sunday was filmed by the press and aired on TV that night to almost 50 million Americans. Anger spread across the country, starting sit-ins and protests nationwide in favor of voting rights for African Americans. *"With the outrage of Selma still fresh,"* President Johnson asked Congress for the swift passage of the voting rights law.

In August 1965, the Voting Rights Act was signed into law. President Johnson promised the government would make sure the law was upheld: *"I pledge you that we will not delay, or we will not hesitate, or we will not turn aside until Americans of every race and color and origin in this country have the same right as all others to share in the process of democracy."*

WHAT DID IT SAY?

Many states had measures in place that kept African Americans from voting. The Voting Rights Act was meant to stop the use of these measures, including making **literacy** tests for voters illegal. The act also set up government oversight of voter registration in places where more than 50 percent of the nonwhite population wasn't registered. Because of the Voting Rights Act of 1965, about 250,000 new black voters registered to vote that year.

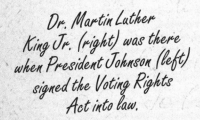

Dr. Martin Luther King Jr. (right) was there when President Johnson (left) signed the Voting Rights Act into law.

BLACK
Nationalism

Not every African American supported the methods and aims of major civil rights groups. Black nationalists believed the United States was an unjust nation to black men and women. They didn't just want their rights. They wanted to separate from whites altogether and create a movement of pride in being black.

By the mid-1960s, many black nationalists were annoyed with the insistence on nonviolence. A leader in the black nationalist movement, Malcolm X, said he didn't want to use violence, but believed African Americans should be able to fight back: *If we could bring about recognition and respect of our people by peaceful means, well and good . . . But I'm also a realist. The only people in this country who are asked to be nonviolent are black people.*

MALCOLM X

Malcolm X began speaking out in favor of civil rights for black Americans in the mid-1950s. He was famous for disagreeing with King's insistence on nonviolence, stating that blacks should be allowed to achieve their goals *"by any means necessary."* He was a leader in a religious and black nationalist group called the Nation of Islam. However, by the mid-1960s, he no longer agreed with their leaders and formed his own group. Soon after, he was assassinated.

Black nationalism grew partly from the work of Marcus Garvey, a Jamaican immigrant who created a group in 1914 that tried to help black Americans live better economically, politically, and socially.

Malcolm X (left) helped change the terms used to refer to African Americans from "Negro" and "colored" to "black" and "Afro-American." Black nationalist sayings included "black power" and "black is beautiful."

THE FALL
of a King

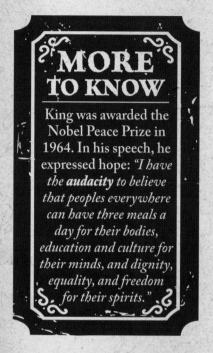
King had become the face of the civil rights movement in the 1960s. He began planning the Poor People's Campaign, a protest to demand jobs, a fair minimum wage, and education for poor adults and children. However, on April 4, 1968, King was shot and killed in Memphis, Tennessee, by a man named James Earl Ray. April 7, 1968, was named a national day of mourning for King.

Nonetheless, the movement continued. Thousands headed to Washington in May as part of the Poor People's Campaign, camping on the National Mall for 6 weeks and protesting the treatment of the poor. As Reverend Samuel "Billy" Kyles, a long-time civil rights activist who was present when King was shot, said: *"You can kill the dreamer. But you cannot kill the dream."*

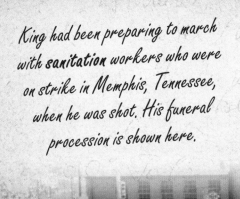

King had been preparing to march with *sanitation* workers who were on strike in Memphis, Tennessee, when he was shot. His funeral procession is shown here.

The night before he was killed, Martin Luther King Jr. said to a crowd: *"I've seen the promised land. I may not get there with you. But I want you to know tonight that we, as a people, will get to the promised land."* His death seemed to reflect to some that nonviolence would only achieve so much. **Riots** and conflicts exploded in over 100 cities. Forty-three people were killed, thousands were injured, and thousands more were arrested.

An ONGOING *Movement*

By the end of the 1960s, both King and Malcolm X had been assassinated. Civil rights laws had been passed, and Jim Crow seemed to have been conquered. However, segregation continued in numerous cities, with many African Americans still living in poor, urban areas. Despite the ruling of *Brown v. Board of Education*, some schools were forced to **integrate** with the assistance of US military. In some areas, integration never really happened. During the 1970s and 1980s, civil rights leaders spent time defending and strengthening the laws and gains made in the 1960s.

BUILDING ON THE '60S

The Civil Rights Act of 1964 was just the first federal act won by the civil rights movement. Several others, including voting rights acts that extended protections, have been passed since. The Civil Rights Act of 1968, or Fair Housing Act, banned discrimination in housing based on race, sex, religion, and national origin. The Civil Rights Restoration Act passed in 1988 made antidiscrimination laws apply to every part of an organization if any part receives government funds.

The *Washington Post* reported that Rosa Parks commented on the continued struggle in 1998: *"Racism is still with us. But it is up to us to prepare our children for what they have to meet, and, hopefully, we shall overcome."*

MORE TO KNOW

In 1969, the 13 African American members of the House of Representatives formed the Congressional Black Caucus. The group's goal is to give a voice in Congress to all African Americans and overlooked groups.

Jesse Jackson, a longtime civil rights activist, made historic runs to become the Democratic presidential nominee in 1984 and 1988.

In 2014, Barack Obama, the first black US president, said: *"Because of the civil rights movement, new doors of opportunity and education swung open for everybody . . . They swung open for you, and they swung open for me."* The civil rights movement lives on, as do its struggles. Racially motivated crimes make headlines, and protests against discrimination continue. In 2013, the Supreme Court struck down a part of the Voting Rights Act that forbade states with a history of discrimination to change voting laws without federal oversight. Many worry about fair voting laws.

Civil rights leader Dorothy Height summed up the future of the movement while encouraging involvement of all races: *"We have to recognize that we have a long way to go, but we have to go that way together."*

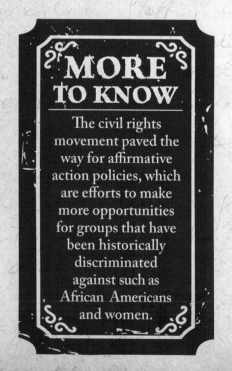

MORE TO KNOW

The civil rights movement paved the way for affirmative action policies, which are efforts to make more opportunities for groups that have been historically discriminated against such as African Americans and women.

TIMELINE

CIVIL RIGHTS MOVEMENT
OF THE 1950s AND 1960s

1954 — The Supreme Court rules on *Brown v. Board of Education of Topeka*.

1955 — Rosa Parks refuses to give up her seat on the bus.

1955 — The Montgomery bus boycott begins.

1956 — The Montgomery bus boycott ends with the desegregation of the bus system.

1957 — Dr. Martin Luther King Jr. and others form the Southern Christian Leadership Conference.

1960 — Four students stage the first sit-in in Greensboro, North Carolina.

1961 — The Freedom Rides begin.

1963 — King, in jail in Birmingham, writes "Letter from Birmingham City Jail."

1963 — More than 200,000 people join the March on Washington for Jobs and Freedom.

1964 — President Lyndon Johnson signs the Civil Rights Act of 1964.

1964 — King wins the Nobel Peace Prize.

1965 — Malcolm X is assassinated.

1965 — Police and civil rights activists clash on Bloody Sunday.

1965 — The Voting Rights Act of 1965 is signed into law.

1968 — King is assassinated.

LEADERS TURNED POLITICIANS

One way leaders of the civil rights movement continue to make a difference today is by running for office. In addition to Jesse Jackson and John Lewis, many have become governors, members of Congress, and more. Andrew Young, another early civil rights leader, went on to represent Georgia in Congress, serve as a US ambassador, and was mayor of Atlanta, Georgia. In 2017, the Congressional Black Caucus had the most members in its history at 49.

GLOSSARY

activist: a person who uses or supports strong actions to help make changes in politics or society

assassinate: to kill someone, especially a public figure

audacity: the state of being bold or sure

boycott: to refuse to have dealings with a person or business in order to force change

discrimination: unfairly treating people unequally because of their race or beliefs

inherently: having to do with the main structure of something

integrate: to make a smaller group part of a larger group

literacy: the ability to read something and answer questions about it

ratify: to give formal approval to something

riot: a public disturbance during which a group of angry people become noisy and out of control

sanitation: the process of keeping places free from dirt, infection, and disease by removing waste

segregate: to force separation of races or classes

violate: to do harm to or break

FOR MORE
Information

Books

Deal, Heidi. *Perspectives on the Civil Rights Movement.* Mankato, MN: 12 Story Library, 2018.

Hooks, Gwendolyn. *If You Were a Kid During the Civil Rights Movement.* New York, NY: Children's Press, 2017.

Mahoney, Emily Jankowski. *American Civil Rights Movement.* New York, NY: PowerKids Press, 2017.

Websites

Civil Rights
www.brainpop.com/socialstudies/ushistory/civilrights/
Watch a short video that summarizes the American civil rights movement.

Civil Rights Movements
www.historyforkids.net/civil-rights.html
Find out about civil rights leaders from all over the world.

Martin Luther King Speech: "I Have a Dream"
www.schooltube.com/video/bcef4580516f12afcad4/
Watch actual footage of Martin Luther King Jr. giving his famous speech at the March on Washington.

INDEX